ARKANSAS IS

FIGHTING CANCER

ONE POEM A DAY

BOOKS BY Dr. Owen Watson

Prayers for Life's Journey

Betting on Me: Revelatory Concepts for Success

Po' Man Ain't Got Not Much Say

What Matters Most: Family, Friends, and Foes

ARKANSAS IS FIGHTING CANCER ONE POEM A DAY

By Dr. Owen Watson

TURN THE PAGE
IN YOUR LIFE

First Edition

Cover Design By: Dr. Owen Watson

Library of Congress Cataloging-in-Publication Data

ISBN-13: 978-1-7331641-8-4

Dedication

T his book is dedicated to my great friend, Stephen Schoenleber, who succumbed to cancer at 9:15 a.m. on March 11, 2013. Although we were a world apart in spiritual beliefs, we did share a kindred spirit of intellect, fun, and friendship that fused us as brothers. We had many shameless times together, to include dancing with one another to the playing of "Ebony and Ivory" in an open mall located in Tel Aviv, Israel, May 1996. Typing this dedication brings back many joyful memories of our friendship and sorrowful tears about his demise. It's in his honor that a piece of our brotherly love for one another is shared to combat cancer, encourage others, and bring hope for a cure soon.

A friendship developed
by unguided chance;
We formed a bond
in song and dance

You were an inspiration,
full of ideas and talent;
Always determined
and a fighter who was ever valiant

Though we appreciated life
while travelling different paths,
we were always mindful of each other
sharing good times and laughs

A dear friend you were,
now flying beyond the moon;
I'll forever cherish thoughts of my friend
who is gone too soon!

"Finally, brothers and sisters, whatever is true, whatever is noble, whatever is right, whatever is pure, whatever is lovely, whatever is admirable – if anything is excellent or praiseworthy – think about such things."

-Holy Bible, NIV, Philippians 4:8

Table of Contents

Arkansas' State Motto

"Regnat Populus"
[The People Rule]

We have indifferences and
to live with one another we must;
Yet, we unify in times of need
against anything that's a threat to us

Cancer seems prevalent and
to fight it alone is the mind of a fool;
In unity we shall triumph over it
because we are the people who rule!

~Dr. Owen Watson~
Chief Petty Officer (retired), U.S. Navy

Arkansas' State Flower

Apple Blossom

Acknowledgements

In honor of Tracy Strop
(recognized by Natasha King)

In honor of Shannon Taylor
(recognized by Natasha King)

In honor of Annie Rainey
(recognized by Anna Jones)

In honor of Thomas Rainey Sr.
(recognized by Brenda Cohen)

In honor of Shaun Carter
(recognized by Gene Carter)

In honor of Andre Welch
(recognized by Dr. Owen Watson)

In honor of Doris C. Davis
(recognized by Ramona Watson)

In honor of Dorothy Rainey
(recognized by Leamorica Watson)

In honor of Alma Jenkins
(recognized by Beatrice Davis)

In honor of Tameka Johnson
(recognized by Terry Curl)

In honor of Anna Jones
(recognized by Dr. Owen Watson)

In honor of Thomas Mullins
(recognized by Tammara Mullins)

In honor of Deborah Rainey
(recognized by Anna Jones)

In honor of Gwendolyn Redfield-Thomas
(recognized by JoAnn Johnson)

In honor of Nancy Valentin
(recognized by Miguel Ortiz)

In honor of Michael Ward
(recognized by Dr. Owen Watson)

In honor of Leamorica Watson
(recognized by Dr. Owen Watson)

In honor of Jeremiah Wilson
(recognized by Shontay Bond)

In honor of Dorothy Rainey
(recognized by Irma Curington)

In honor of Andre Welch
(recognized by Dr. Owen Watson)

Introduction

C ancer has been running rampant for many years, but it is in the process of losing its steam. There have been numerous prayers along with many funds and much support in every way contributing to destroy its very existence. Until a cure is found - and it will be discovered - it is vital that we all find a way to help combat the ill-effects it has on victims and their loved ones world-wide. We can do so by offering encouragement, spreading love, and inspiring hope. That is exactly what this book is designed to do, fight cancer one poem a day!

I AM, I CAN
Day 1

An inspiration to others,
I arise from the perception of condemned;
A vibrant spirit thriving within,
manifests the true I am

Living beyond the sorrows of many,
sometimes in thought as my only fan;
I faithfully recognize the power of prayer,
courageously overcoming all, I can!

RIGHT NOW, RIGHT HERE
Day 2

The joy I have within
is truly like none other;
I am so blessed to be me,
a picture of love uncovered

Time is never of the essence,
when you have a duty to bring cheer;
Always give your best,
right now, right here!

TURN THE PAGE
IN YOUR LIFE

NEVER OUT
Day 3

This thing called life
has simply just begun;
Never mind the number of years ahead,
capitalize on embracing every second of fun

Silly faces, funny stories,
let's spread smiles all about;
Creating cherished memories,
like a never-ending game of baseball,
you're always at bat and never out!

MY SONG
Day 4

Unique can best describe me,
for I am truly one of a kind;
A pattern of glory
etched in a most valuable design

With my confidence
I'm a sure bet to get the gong;
as I share and teach others
how to believe in themselves, sing, and live my song!

TURN THE PAGE
IN YOUR LIFE

GOOD PAIN
Day 5

When I'm in pain,
it's good to have your support;
Steadily offering encouraging words,
beyond the medical report

You say I'm your strength,
the bright sun beaming through dark clouds of
thunder, lightning and rain;
Yet, I say it's you
who turns my excruciating to my good pain!

THE CHANGE
Day 6

Sympathy is not what's being sought,
however, it's nice to know I'm in your thought;
Although appreciation can never be bought,
I'm ever grateful of the joy you brought

Sometimes I view it as strange,
how all things can be perfectly arranged;
Beyond the scope of my visual range
Someone's life I've touched for the better
has been changed!

TURN THE PAGE
IN YOUR LIFE

THE STAND
Day 7

It's a new day and all is well,
no worries about today's demands;
I am much stronger than yesterday,
being more than able to stand

I am an expression of love,
willing to share beyond the hand;
The love I receive is the love I give,
that'll able you as well to stand!

HERE AM I
Day 8

At times when my faith seems to fail,
and I wish to give up with a goodbye;
A still small voice rises up within,
being the Lord saying "Here Am I"

Strength I then receive to continue on
and a renewed spirit to match my battle cry;
For greater is He living within
reminding me "Here Am I"

TURN THE PAGE
IN YOUR LIFE

THE CHAMP
Day 9

Hailing from a family of love and support,
weighing in at double digit pounds;
Heavily equipped with faith,
to overcome all forms of illness ever found

Arising each day,
ready to conquer and feeling amped;
As my supporters proudly sound off
with "here comes the champ!"

LOOKING UP
Day 10

What a day, what a day!
It's filled with laughter and love;
There is much to be thankful for,
as my faith keeps me risen above

Never a day taken for granted,
neither shall negative rule my day abrupt;
For I have an inner strength
that overcomes all,
as I continue looking up

TURN THE PAGE
IN YOUR LIFE

A NOTE
Day 11

So much support
from everyone all around;
Keeps me smiling,
never having to wear a frown

What touches my heart most
is something someone wrote;
Taking time to think of me &
putting it in a simple note

LIFE
Day 12

It's so precious,
yet, so delicate;
sometimes taken for granted,
sometimes many forget

Best to do
instead of being distracted by strife,
appreciate everyday
as you continue to enjoy life!

TURN THE PAGE
IN YOUR LIFE

HIS LOVE
Day 13

To be at peace
is to have peace;
which can only come from
the True One above

So much He must give
just as He has already given;
and, that's this magical thing
called love!

I BELIEVE
Day 14

I believe
better days start everyday;
I believe
my words are heard when I pray

I believe
in the power of the words I say;
I believe
doors will open for all to be okay!

TURN THE PAGE
IN YOUR LIFE

STRONGER
Day 15

Strength I have
to get beyond today;
Strength I have
to heave love toward others way

Strength I have
to live life longer;
Strength I have
as my faith gets stronger

SEEING GOD
Day 16

Oftentimes I've wondered
just how You look;
Until I read the pages
of the greatest book

I now see You everyday
and greet You with a nod;
You're part of everyone around me
who expresses the character of God!

TURN THE PAGE
IN YOUR LIFE

CHILD OF LOVE
Day 17

Child of Love,
is just who you are;
Created in the beginning of time,
placed here from afar

Child of Love,
with purpose to fulfill;
Presenting and sharing your nature
at the Father's will!

SAY YOU
Day 18

I got this,
for nothing can keep me down;
Out of the dirt I'm made,
yet, I have dominion over the ground

Knowing who I know,
I stand firm in what is true;
Realizing nothing can harm me,
because of what say You!

TURN THE PAGE
IN YOUR LIFE

WHAT I KNOW
Day 19

What I know,
I can't always explain;
But as sure as I am here today,
I will press through the pain

What I know,
is the love and support I receive;
They give me the fight of faith
to trust in God, whom I believe!

THE ANSWER
Day 20

The how, when, what, where, and why,
in this lifetime, we may never know;
Yet, we must continue in faith,
as He instructs us so

We seek cures and solutions
to the havoc wreaked by cancer;
Let us not fall short of seeking Him first,
The Answer!

TURN THE PAGE
IN YOUR LIFE

WINGS
Day 21

Look at me,
I'm flying high every day;
The daily smile I share,
is proof of what I say

Look at me,
I'm overjoyed beyond material things;
My spirit is far above in heaven,
soaring without need of wings!

NEVER GOODBYE
Day 22

We're always connected,
regardless of what may happen in the natural;
We were allotted time to bond,
at a pace set by Him gradual

Seeing me now,
is likened to eternity beyond the sky;
For the memories we have,
keep us from ever saying goodbye!

TURN THE PAGE
IN YOUR LIFE

STAND ALL TIME
Day 23

A thousand years may past,
filled with millions of stories untold;
Leaving nothing to ever compare,
to the valued bond we forever hold

Complimenting one another,
with our lives intertwined;
What we have is something unique,
that will surely stand all time!

ATMOSPHERE
Day 24

The power of positivity is all around,
as seen on everyone's face so clear;
No worries in the world,
for love is in the atmosphere

It's a winning day ahead,
giving way for all to cheer;
In unity we can appreciate,
this free gift of love in the atmosphere!

TURN THE PAGE
IN YOUR LIFE

BUCKLE UP
Day 25

What a wild ride in this life,
that many are having to endure;
Prayers sent up daily,
for a much-needed miracle cure

The answer received,
is to share the love that overflows from my cup;
With problems being ever-present,
we must in faith buckle up!

NO STRINGS
Day 26

No matter the situation,
bonds of stress will not control me;
I am doing much better
in His trusted hands faithfully

Living life to the fullest,
no strings to prevent me;
The freedom I'm privileged to enjoy,
He has made possible to be!

TURN THE PAGE
IN YOUR LIFE

KIND WORD
Day 27

It can change the outlook
of any bad situation;
It can make everyday
a grand celebration

In times when needed,
it brings life to much unheard;
It's the simplest thing to give,
take time to spread a kind word!

MINOR SORROW
Day 28

Day after day,
it's my faith that keeps me on the go;
Blessed by His strength,
I'm able to withstand the minor sorrow

The best is here today,
displacing all worries about tomorrow;
The support I have from You,
supersedes my condition of minor sorrow!

TURN THE PAGE
IN YOUR LIFE

MORE THAN
Day 29

More than pain,
More than worry;
More of Your love
becomes my story

More than pity,
More than on my own;
More of family and friends,
proves I'm not in this alone!

DO SAY
Day 30

Do say,
I'm feeling better than ever;
Do say,
giving up will I never

Do say,
life is sweeter everyday;
Do say,
all is possible when you pray!

TURN THE PAGE
IN YOUR LIFE

PROTECTED
Day 31

Troubles may come,
but shall never prevail;
I am protected in His hands,
which guarantee no fail

Though sometimes I am down,
I can never be counted out;
The protection He provides,
brings me beyond any doubt!

FREEDOM FAITH
Day 32

I show love,
I am at peace;
I spread joy,
it shall never cease

Freedom faith
is what I have;
No boundaries or lack,
freedom faith is my path!

TURN THE PAGE
IN YOUR LIFE

THE SAME
Day 33

Yesterday is what it was,
bye-bye to regrets and blame;
I'm living for today,
putting my woes to shame

For there is strength
enabling a better me that cannot be tamed;
The blessed assurance I have,
won't allow me to ever be the same!

THE TESTIMONY
Day 34

Why me?
That's a question I used to ask;
Until I realized
everyone is born with a meaningful task

Sure, I have thoughts about
how life could be;
I've learned to embrace my life
as a wonderful testimony

TURN THE PAGE
IN YOUR LIFE

AM I
Day 35

Am I that someone
who brings joy to your life;
who brightens your day,
beyond life's strife?

Am I that someone
you pray for without a doubt;
knowing that He hears and answers,
trusting it will all work out?

SMILEY TIME
Day 36

Pictures help so much
in remembering loved ones as they are;
Just as reminiscent thoughts,
they bring healing to whatever life's scar

Take advantage of the moment,
know that it is never a crime;
To make memorable frames,
during this smiley time

TURN THE PAGE
IN YOUR LIFE

MADE TOUGH
Day 37

There is nothing stronger
that I'm unable to bear;
For God gives me the strength
because He lovingly cares

Whenever I have thoughts
of enough is enough;
He reminds me through family and friends
how I am made tough!

CHARGING YOU
Day 38

So much support I've received
from many family and friends;
There's no way to repay
or close gaps of loose ends

However, my gratitude is shown
by what I ask each to do;
Love one another and others the same,
is my charge to you!

TURN THE PAGE
IN YOUR LIFE

NO KIDDING
Day 39

No kidding of any kind,
I am really doing just fine;
No kidding of any kind,
I am blessed with you in mind

No kidding of any kind,
I can overcome any grind;
No kidding of any kind,
nothing shall keep me in a bind

THE DESIRE
Day 40

What I have
burns inside like a flame of fire;
Not of harm but of passion,
as it is my heart's desire

To continue influencing many,
beyond life's circumstances so dire;
Think of me and realize,
you are fulfilling my desire!

TURN THE PAGE
IN YOUR LIFE

WELL DONE
Day 41

What I am here to do
is to introduce joy in your world;
To play games, share jokes,
and prank other boys and girls

Live, love, and laugh,
all in the name of fun;
These are most valuable memories,
as we look to hear "Well Done!"

OBSERVE ME
Day 42

Up and about,
never counted out;
This is how I'd like it to be,
living my life for all to see

Embrace me as I am,
not in pain and agony;
I want to be your inspiration,
So, I ask that you observe me

TURN THE PAGE
IN YOUR LIFE

BLESSED
Day 43

Blessed, I am
Blessed, you see
Blessed, I can
Blessed, are we

Blessed for today
Blessed in my condition
Blessed for tomorrow
Blessed according to God's vision!

GREATER THAN I
Day 44

I have a higher hope,
I experience a stronger love;
I give thanks to the Higher One,
who reigns among us and from above

I find relief against all
that happens under the sky;
For He's in control,
He is much greater than I!

TURN THE PAGE
IN YOUR LIFE

BEAUTIFUL RAIN
Day 45

Magnificence is all around,
even seen throughout nature;
We mustn't bypass the opportunity
to appreciate it without cost or wager

There's nothing like simple things
that take away hurt and pain;
Bumble bees buzzing, swaying trees, or
the gentle falling beautiful rain

HIS MIGHT
Day 46

We all face struggles and fears
and at times we may have to fight;
Yet, we conquer them all
by the power of His might

His presence allows for a future
that is ever so bright;
He makes a way for our path of joy
by the power of His might

TURN THE PAGE
IN YOUR LIFE

MASTER'S PEACE
Day 47

It's unspeakable
It's unimaginable
It's something only He can give
and it's not tangible

It can't be bought
nor can it be leased;
It's given without charge,
Just ask and accept the Master's peace

THIS DAY
Day 48

Glad to be alive
this day
Glad to make a positive impact
this day

Glad to inspire others
this day
Glad you are a part of my life
this day

TURN THE PAGE
IN YOUR LIFE

GREATEST GIFT
Day 49

Beholding those who surround me,
who pick me up when I need a lift;
They represent the arms of God,
delivering to me His greatest gift

When worry seeks to distract me,
at times in my mind causing a rift;
He sends those family and friends
to remind me that they are His greatest gift

MORNING
Day 50

Looking ahead to a better tomorrow,
the morning will soon arrive;
Readying myself to spread the love
so that others too may thrive

A new day is a new beginning
that each morning brings;
Another opportunity to appreciate
the love and support for all things

TURN THE PAGE
IN YOUR LIFE

NO PAY
Day 51

Nothing owed but much is given
to keep everyone looking positively ahead;
Something sowed but not for gain,
a product of kind words said

Freely, much is distributed
among the caring at hand;
No pay offered for doing
what only prayer and God can

ALL FOR YOU
Day 52

You're worth the time
You're worth the celebration
You're beautifully kind
You're love in manifestation

You're worth the overnight stays
You're worth the day long talks
You're the one who makes our days
I enjoy your company in the walks

TURN THE PAGE
IN YOUR LIFE

GOOD FEELING
Day 53

Today is sort of special,
why, I can't explain;
However, I know for sure,
blessings are to come like rain

The sensation being felt
is not hope I'm stealing;
It's a supernatural power within
that is sparking this good feeling

CONVENIENCE
Day 54

The heart of my condition
is beyond what you could see;
For the state I'm physically in,
is only a shell of me

Inside I am very vibrant,
with a heart of resilience;
No need to feel sorry for me,
I'm seizing mental convenience

TURN THE PAGE
IN YOUR LIFE

CHRISTOPHANY
Day 55

In so many ways
You have been revealed
through family and friends who comfort me
fulfilling Your will

I say thank You
for making Yourself known
a Christophany of hosts you sent
never leaving me alone

BLUE SKIES
Day 56

The thrill of looking up
is the beauty to be seen
The greatness and wonders
reality beyond a dream

Nature empowers me
to dig deep and rise
Better days are coming to enjoy
more blue skies

TURN THE PAGE
IN YOUR LIFE

READY TO GO
Day 57

This place I call home
can at times be so lonely;
Thinking no one understands
I'm the one fighting, only

When I arise from self-pity
and glorified sorrow
I accept this day in appreciation,
ready to go on to a brighter tomorrow

THE FLIGHT
Day 58

There's no limit
to what can be done
My expectations are without borders
because I trust in the Almighty One

My thoughts are on high
as I walk by faith not sight
I am totally prepared to demonstrate
with a testimony that'll surely take flight

TURN THE PAGE
IN YOUR LIFE

HOME
Day 59

There's a place within
that provides room for me to live free
I call it my home
where I visualize a better me

Those who are welcomed,
I invite you in with cheer
Greeted with a smile, love
and in my eyes, you see no fear

YOU'RE THERE
Day 60

Whenever I go to sleep
Whenever I awake
You're there
my relief from every ache

You're there just because
you love me so much
I shall treasure all you offer
with a firm heartfelt clutch

TURN THE PAGE
IN YOUR LIFE

MY MIND
Day 61

The mind can wander
on any- and everything amiss;
Be strong and stand your guard,
you have the power to resist

Set your mind on course,
toward that which is healthy and wise;
Give no thought to destruction
and accept no facade of lies

A TIME
Day 62

Once upon a time
I had dreams beyond belief
On track to accomplish them all
until I was smitten with grief

But I know
this is only a season;
Better is to come,
this is only a set time with reason

TURN THE PAGE
IN YOUR LIFE

BEING ALONE
Day 63

Something I've rarely considered
is the idea of being alone
When the thought would cross my mind
I'd just toss it away like a stone

I have many who care about me,
steady by my side night and day
Being alone isn't something I have to cope
when I have love coming from every way

NEVER IMAGINED
Day 64

This thing that has come upon me
tires me out oftentimes
It's something I'd wish upon no one,
hoping one day a cure they find

Yet, I'd never imagined
this was to be my lowest point of living
I will turn it around for the positive
to share with others the precious time I'm given

TURN THE PAGE
IN YOUR LIFE

SETTLE DOWN
Day 65

With so much going on,
life can be a bit of an uproar
Take a deep breath and listen to a song,
behind you close the door

Never lose your cool,
letting yourself run aground
Regain your peace within,
always take a moment to settle down

FOREVER
Day 66

Nights seem long,
days seem so short;
Waiting on what you're going through
to end in an abort

I will not fall short
nor give up never;
I know this is temporary,
not to last forever

TURN THE PAGE
IN YOUR LIFE

MY SAVIOR
Day 67

I know someone
able to overcome it all
He'll restore your losses,
be a safety net when you fall

Trust in Him
with an enthusiastic behavior
Let me introduce you to my friend
Jesus, my savior

EVERY JOURNEY
Day 68

Everyone's journey
will hit some sort of snag
Don't gather unneeded objects,
only carry what is needed in your bag

Journeys are to be traveled,
requiring special attention
Dare to be distracted,
stay focused on the mission

TURN THE PAGE
IN YOUR LIFE

MY HERO
Day 69

That everyday friend
that parent, sibling, or other relative
they are those who make
living life imperative

They are the heroes
who save me from drowning in sorrows
They are the heroes
carrying me into better tomorrows

NO PAST
Day 70

Being what it was
I knew forever it wouldn't last
I am ever so grateful
it's become a problem of the past

All things are much brighter
than what could be seen before
With an uplifted head and raised hands
I thank You for closing that door

TURN THE PAGE
IN YOUR LIFE

ONLY DESIRE
Day 71

To be surrounded in love,
by those who are close in heart,
is what I pray to be
early in the morning prior to day start

They keep me from sinking
in the defeat of mire;
I need to have them every day,
this is my only desire

IT'S TRUE
Day 72

It's true,
that I believe the truth
The battle is not mine to fight,
victory declared before my youth

It's true,
that my faith is steadfast
Though it is but a measure,
In His mighty hand, is where my care is cast

TURN THE PAGE
IN YOUR LIFE

KEEP YOU
Day 73

I'm mindful of you
because you are my child
Before you were conceived
I imagined seeing your smile

Just as before you were manifested
I pictured and knew
In memory, in love, in heart,
I will forever keep you

WORLD OF RIGHT
Day 74

Sometimes things we perceive as wrong,
can turn out to be right
Let's not cast aside the workings going on
because we can't accept them with our sight

It takes the bad road for some
to bring purpose into existence
That's the world we live in,
some with and some without resistance

TURN THE PAGE
IN YOUR LIFE

WHISTLE
Day 75

A simple whistle
can become the song you need
Wondering to yourself,
if God has heard you plead

Within that whistle,
a whisper can be heard
"You have my favor",
with that, my spirit is renewed and stirred

OPEN HAND
Day 76

What's in an open hand?
I hope it's what many can use;
Not for selfish gain,
nor to be taken for granted or abused

The open hand that many seek,
when it appears hope is gone,
is one that presents encouragement,
reviving strength to carry on

TURN THE PAGE
IN YOUR LIFE

MY REPORT
Day 77

Some days are good,
some days are bad;
I maintain a positive focus
to deter being sad

Though the report
is subject to change;
I keep my spirit well-fed
all words of affirmation without range

RELIEF
Day 78

A little something is needed
to ease the pain;
Especially during those times alone,
in a state of disdain

Then comes you by my side,
to uplift me from grief;
Encouraging me with your presence,
providing me a moment of relief

TURN THE PAGE
IN YOUR LIFE

WHOLE
Day 79

Broken but not defeated,
my spirit is indestructible;
Though part of me is crippled,
I'm not beyond repairable

That which is inside
will enable me to attain the goal;
Living a full and long life,
physically and spiritually whole

365
Day 80

There is no 365
without there first being a one;
To live life day by day,
thankful for each that has begun

A day of life
is a gift from on high;
Purposing each of us to
live, love, laugh...365

TURN THE PAGE
IN YOUR LIFE

DAYS COUNT
Day 81

Some may count you out,
by what they see, read, or hear;
Some may start the countdown,
with trembling and fear

A few may count you in,
because they look beyond;
They're the ones making days count,
cheering "fight, crawl, walk, run!"

MY WAY
Day 82

If I had it my way with one wish,
illnesses would never exist;
We'd all live healthy lives,
not ever having a need to persist

Then again, having it anyone's way
doesn't resolve reasons for hate and the lack of love;
That stems from everyone having it their way,
disregarding perfect instructions from above

TURN THE PAGE
IN YOUR LIFE

FAVORED
Day 83

I am alive,
this day;
Grateful,
in every way

I am alive,
life is savored;
All needs met
in Him, I'm favored

TOUCHING LIVES
Day 84

There's a touch,
as though directly from heaven;
It's like a piece of God's love,
keeping you going 24/7

That touch is given
by those around through it all;
With unfailing support,
others enabling me to stand straight and tall

TURN THE PAGE
IN YOUR LIFE

NEED ME
Day 85

There are times I feel worthless,
don't want to hope no more;
I just want to throw in the towel,
on the future close the door

Then I hear a small voice saying,
'let go of the lies and self-pity';
Awakened, I realize there's more to live for
such as others who need me

AFTER WHILE
Day 86

I view life as the latter being now,
so I choose to live fully today;
Some may ask why and how?
My answer is simply by His grace

I will give and share what is needed,
be it a hug, touch, or coy smile;
I will not waste the day
believing I can do it sometime after while

TURN THE PAGE
IN YOUR LIFE

YELLOW ROOM
Day 87

Everyone should have a special place
where they can go to get away;
An escape from the troubles of life
and the worries of the day

My special dwelling just happens to be
nothing spectacular as bang, bam, boom,
it's a little quiet and peaceful place,
that I like to call my yellow room

DAYLIGHT
Day 88

Darkness holds no power
over what shines bright;
My hopes, dreams, strength
fuels me through each passing night

Darkness tries to provide
a state of hopelessness and fright;
I rise above it all
encapsulated in the daylight

TURN THE PAGE
IN YOUR LIFE

CONSTELLATION
Day 89

Far above,
as the naked eye can see,
are designs that provide hope;
coordinated by His majesty

Just as the stars are set in order,
no flaw to be found at all,
rest assure that on Him
I shall trust and forever call

COMPLETE
Day 90

Brokenness
is not the end of this story;
It only serves in producing
a greater testimony to His glory

In life,
many things can knock us off our feet;
The significance of faith
is knowing we are overcomers and complete

TURN THE PAGE
IN YOUR LIFE

LOVE
Day 91

What is it
that comforts at all times,
unfailing,
pure and divine,
unchanging,
always above the line,
to be given
ready and prime?
Love

CHARITY
Day 92

From the heart,
is when it counts;
Timely given,
no shame nor doubt

Precious and priceless,
as a treasure to behold;
Is the love and joy you give,
the greatest story ever told

TURN THE PAGE
IN YOUR LIFE

JOY
Day 93

There's a certain beauty
one can appreciate;
Such as unspeakable joy,
expressing faith not fate

Things around may be chaotic,
continuing on without good in sight;
The inner rising of His joy prevails,
knowing the war is His to fight

PEACE
Day 94

The storms are quieted,
as peace is maintained;
Trusting in Him
erases the pain

Pressing forward,
doing the least;
He takes your burden,
as He gives you His peace

TURN THE PAGE
IN YOUR LIFE

GENTLENESS
Day 95

Opening a door,
allowing others to proceed first;
Giving a cup of water
to one who thirsts

Putting faith on feet,
places yourself last in mind;
Yet, there's honor in doing good,
representing God by being kind

LONG-SUFFERING
Day 96

In spite of it all,
I remain standing;
Sometimes thoughts of giving up arise,
when treatments are demanding

"How much longer can I last?"
Is the question most asked;
The thought fades away
upon realizing I'm built for the task

TURN THE PAGE
IN YOUR LIFE

FAITHFULNESS
Day 97

Though attempted by many,
no one can compare;
You are faithful to your word,
to everyone everywhere

None but You
can lift me from where I am;
In You I shall trust,
for You are faithful to the lion and the lamb

SELF-CONTROL
Day 98

Losing my mind
is so easy to do;
I must stay grounded
and walk alongside you

Lies unhinge me,
trying to get a foothold;
Nonetheless,
Your spirit grants me self-control

TURN THE PAGE
IN YOUR LIFE

GOODNESS
Day 99

There is none good but One,
in Him shall I abide;
Stepping out on my own,
would simply be my pride

What I seek
is not a hope of 'would';
With unshakeable faith,
I will experience His offering of good

THE POSITIVE
Day 100

You see the shape I am in
You see a condition
You see a state of distress
But it's part of a greater mission

You see me happy
You see me doing my best
You see I have a life to live
It is faith that makes you positive

TURN THE PAGE
IN YOUR LIFE

NO NEGATIVE REPORT
Day 101

Shall I run, give up or in
to fear?
Shall I stop having hope,
and accept death is near?

Such thoughts
I'm choosing to thwart;
His word cancels
the negative report

THINKING
Day 102

We're at home
enjoying life better than before;
Going to the movies, running errands,
having fun galore

Appreciating the gift of life,
tea, soda, and water we sit drinking;
Soon this will all become real
beyond wishful thinking

TURN THE PAGE
IN YOUR LIFE

BEAUTIFUL
Day 103

An offer of trading places
displays love abound;
It lets one know
in your heart they are found

What is seen in the natural,
can be shunned by some;
Through the Son-glasses,
beauty is seen and welcomed

DINNERTIME
Day 104

The layout looks great
with a salad of grace;
Appreciating the bread of life,
joy on my face;
Nothing can beat
an entrée of love;
Water provided in the form of Spirit,
a delightful dessert of heaven above
It's dinnertime!

TURN THE PAGE
IN YOUR LIFE

RESPONSIBLE
Day 105

The state I'm in,
I shift no blame;
The culprit is a liar
and cancer is the name

How I am to be,
many believe is impossible;
The testimony is coming forth
by the One Whom my faith holds responsible

THE PLAN
Day 106

If I was in charge,
this would've never happened to me;
Love doesn't position someone
to live a life painfully

In silence,
I start to understand;
Complaining only prolongs
His greater plan

TURN THE PAGE
IN YOUR LIFE

NO QUESTIONS
Day 107

I have a right
to rant and question "Why me?";
I am often asked,
"Why you?" by friends and family

Questions upon questions
with no viable answers to provide;
Maybe quietness is the answer
with trust in Him, I shall abide

CALL ME, PLEASE
Day 108

I appreciate you being there
when things are going good;
But it's when I need you most,
there to be I wish you could

I wait patiently for hearing your voice,
to put my spirit at ease;
Although I have thoughts of us together,
it would really help if you call Me [God], please

TURN THE PAGE
IN YOUR LIFE

REMEMBER ME
Day 109

Let me not ever be
an after-thought;
May I be a constant memory
as a victor of the battle fought

Uplifting and leading the way,
you have the victory;
If you're ever feeling defeated,
relax and remember me

STORMY NIGHTS
Day 110

Stormy nights,
here for a moment
Stormy nights,
very unwanted
Stormy nights,
aren't the end
Stormy nights,
reveals your friend

TURN THE PAGE
IN YOUR LIFE

DARK DAYS
Day 111

Through it all,
there's something to look forward to;
The darkness only covers
what is truly meant for you

You must be patient,
for the light will soon come;
As a beacon of hope,
you'll share the breakthrough with some

NO HOPE
Day 112

What is this
that has come upon me?
I'm here,
feeling so helplessly

To my feet I will stand,
living beyond just to cope;
I have others who believe in me,
no reason to ever lose hope

TURN THE PAGE
IN YOUR LIFE

IN PLAIN SIGHT
Day 113

Angry and in despair,
trying to hold on and maintain;
Smiling around others,
when alone, I wallow in my pain

With eyes open,
I am encouraged through the night;
When thoughts of loved ones' care
is evident in plain sight

PRECOCIOUS ONE
Day 114

Is it because of my education,
that I'm viewed as such?
Could it be how persistent I am
by the hearts and lives I touch?

If you must know,
it's not by my doing at all how I am able to have fun;
It's because of the spirit given to me
by the ultimate Precocious One

TURN THE PAGE
IN YOUR LIFE

SINCERE
Day 115

Before it was ever realized,
you were closer then, just as you are now;
You've always been a friend,
without attempting to figure out how

Your loyalty and respect
is what I'll forever hold dear;
There's nothing comparable
to a friendship that is sincere

DEAR ME
Day 116

How am I?
I'm doing fine;
Life can be challenging,
but I have a co-sign

A zest for life is how I live,
daily renewed;
I must go for now
and fill up on spiritual food

TURN THE PAGE
IN YOUR LIFE

MAYBE
Day 117

A 'maybe' is good
in certain situations;
It's not that all answers are absolute,
but we must have an anticipation

Maybe if we all
could take a step outside the box;
Maybe we can be further advanced,
instead of weighted in place with the same rocks

I TOLD YOU SO
Day 118

A-ha, I told you so,
I'd see you today;
Because it wasn't
my time to fly away

A-ha, I told you so,
I walk by faith not by doubt;
I have too much to live for,
so it was cancer I had to cast out

TURN THE PAGE
IN YOUR LIFE

YOU'RE THE ONE
Day 119

Who is there beside me,
no matter how terrible things get?
Providing a spring of hope,
in the midst of sickness debt

Putting up with my rants,
rage, and anger;
You're the one who has protected me
from self-danger

EMPATHY
Day 120

Walking in my shoes
is not what I want from you;
This isn't an experience
everyone is guaranteed to get through

Support however you can,
without feeling a need to relate;
That's a powerful show of concern,
without putting stress on your plate

TURN THE PAGE
IN YOUR LIFE

WHAT ABOUT...?
Day 121

What about me?
What about you?
What about us
doing what we do?

Keeping a smile,
making every minute count;
Redeeming the time with unlimited joy
springing from the fount

IS REAL
Day 122

What you see of me,
is but a figment of your imagination;
I need you to look closer and deeper,
to gain the revelation

What you see in me,
is beyond how you perceive I feel;
You see someone strong,
fighting with faith that is real

TURN THE PAGE
IN YOUR LIFE

CAN'T IGNORE THE FACT
Day 123

The facts are there
for all to see;
They oftentimes stumble us
in our belief

Though you can't ignore them,
because of habits from our youth;
You must let go and grab hold of
the Word of truth!

I'M CONVINCED
Day 124

There is something
that encourages me from within;
It is that something
that most find difficult to comprehend

It enables me to stand,
keeps me from being tense;
It provides a vision of me in perfect health
I receive by faith, I'm convinced!

TURN THE PAGE
IN YOUR LIFE

WITHDRAWN
Day 125

I'm so glad
you are yet here,
whereas some fall by the wayside
because of fear

You've been by my side
from dusk til dawn;
I'm blessed with you as a friend
to bring me out, when I feel withdrawn

INTERESTING
Day 126

Interesting,
how others say I should feel,
how I should look,
how I should sit still

Interesting,
how I defy the status quo,
how positive I am,
how I demonstrate the power of Who I know

TURN THE PAGE
IN YOUR LIFE

MY CLAIM
Day 127

My claim of strength
is substantiated in you;
Holding my hand, giving me hugs and kisses
much more than a few

My claim for living
is found within life itself;
To inspire those around
with my clean bill of health

MY ENDORSEMENT
Day 128

Long shall I live
Long shall I be remembered
Long shall I give
Never shall I surrender

Long shall I rejoice
Long shall I maintain the fire
Long shall I use my voice
to always inspire

TURN THE PAGE
IN YOUR LIFE

I WISH YOU
Day 129

A better day,
peace galore,
a joyful heart
and so much more

Know me now,
like you've known me then;
My wish is for you to realize
this isn't the end

I ACCEPT ME
Day 130

You see me as I am,
accept me;
You've known me in a better state,
healthy

I know it gets hard at times
and your heart aches weakly;
What I need from you is to
accept and walk with me

TURN THE PAGE
IN YOUR LIFE

FREE TO BELIEVE
Day 131

I am not bound
by labels placed on me;
I give no thought
to predictions of maybe

I have a choice
to lift up my voice;
So from on high I receive
and by faith I believe

THE QUESTION
Day 132

How do I get beyond this?
Why has this come upon me?
What good can come of this?
I'm tired of waiting to see

Where do I go from here?
What is my confession?
Hold onto faith,
without doubt or question

TURN THE PAGE
IN YOUR LIFE

JUSTIFIABLE
Day 133

The means of overcoming
is by having a testimony;
Bearing adverse conditions
oftentimes, feeling lonely

What it's worth
is far above the moment of pain;
When it's all said and done,
you have a powerful report to proclaim

NO HARM
Day 134

My lashing out
is from the discomfort I experience
Please forgive me
and pray my relief and deliverance

I truly apologize
No need to sound the alarm
I need you so much right now
and will do my best not to harm

TURN THE PAGE
IN YOUR LIFE

HE TOLD ME SO
Day 135

The brighter day is now
The progress has been great
All doubt has subsided
I've been given a clean slate

To those who may not understand
and wonder how am I sure to know;
I spent time with Him and listened
as His still small voice told me so

NO COMPLAINTS
Day 136

"Woe unto me,
look what I'm going through;
No one really cares
and there's nothing they can do"

I can think such negative thoughts,
but because of faith I can't and ain't;
Receiving what I've prayed for,
comes without complaint

TURN THE PAGE
IN YOUR LIFE

CALM DOWN
Day 137

What's going on?
This can't be happening!
How did things go wrong?
This is too challenging!

Up in arms,
negative all around;
Realize that God has this,
so please, calm down

MY EYES SAY IT ALL
Day 138

There's hope,
there's surprise,
there's a dream,
in them there eyes

There's life,
there's highs,
there's a miracle,
in them there eyes

TURN THE PAGE
IN YOUR LIFE

DENIAL

Day 139

It's there,
this I know;
It will not affect my happiness,
I will not let go

It's not denial
that I'm living in;
I simply refuse
to let it win

CREATION

Day 140

Who's the author
of all creation?
I cannot lose,
in His hands is my salvation

I was created
to bring Him glory;
Better get ready
for a most fascinating story

TURN THE PAGE
IN YOUR LIFE

SIMPLE RELIEF
Day 141

A simple smile
A simple visit
A simple joke
A fun-loving spirit

Picks me up
from patches of grief;
You are my
simple relief

EACH ONE
Day 142

That life to live
That person to touch
We need one another
ever so much

Each one
is the welcoming hand;
Each one
supports for another to stand

TURN THE PAGE
IN YOUR LIFE

HERE YOU GO
Day 143

You're here
by my side
as always;
You're trustworthy,
in you I confide
on all days

I reciprocate with a hug
so you'll know
I appreciate you much,
Here you go

CHANGE OF MIND
Day 144

Not looking
to turn back the hands of time;
Not willing
to have a change of mind

Not seeking
what I can't find;
My faith is steadfast in Him,
no need to have a change of mind

TURN THE PAGE
IN YOUR LIFE

CUSTOMIZED
Day 145

Life,
though full of twist and turns,
is a journey
with a need for meaning we desperately yearn

We become equipped
for what is realized
in the process of struggles
that were customized

MAXIMUM PERFORMANCE
Day 146

Giving my all,
which is my best;
Failure is unacceptable,
in this one-life test

Doing what I can,
without reason to withhold,
I must share what's needed with others
living a life that's bold

TURN THE PAGE
IN YOUR LIFE

QUALITY OF LIFE
Day 147

Having what is needed,
to function as required,
is not always what we have within self
but in that someone to be desired

Someone to talk to such as
a parent, friend, husband or wife;
They are those who bring more value to
one's quality of life

KNOW WHAT ELSE?
Day 148

Know what else?
I am going to beat
what is set before me
Know what else?
I am going to rewrite
the new beginning to my story
Know what else?
I for sure
have the victory
This battle is won!

TURN THE PAGE
IN YOUR LIFE

DEVOTION
Day 149

There's none greater
than you, the Most High
There's none stronger
than you, the Almighty
There's none wiser
than you, the Master Planner
There's none more faithful
than you, my Friend

DARE TO LIVE
Day 150

I say 'no' to death,
nor will I allow worry to consume me;
There's a fire inside
stirred up continually

My defense stands secured
in the Author who has life to give;
I'm designed to fight
as a warrior, who dares to live

TURN THE PAGE
IN YOUR LIFE

STABILITY
Day 151

There's no guarantee
in what tomorrow brings;
Yet, we're called to be ready
for life's dire array of things

Go forth with
significant civility
Live your faith
with a steadfast stability

SCARED
Day 152

There's always a level of fear,
when you're dealing with the unknown;
You must remain focused
and never let your cover be blown

You have the fight within
to overcome that which is dared;
Goodbye to fear,
your faith will put an end to being scared

TURN THE PAGE
IN YOUR LIFE

TOMORROW
Day 153

If not today,
it shall be soon;
If not morning or night,
it shall be noon

It is coming,
many folks' faith will grow;
If not today,
the answer will be tomorrow

THE PREMIERE
Day 154

I am the premiere,
I offer something rarely done;
Ditching the hopelessness,
in exchange for faith in the One

I am the premiere
for others to be inspired by,
not because of what I appear to be,
but because of Who healed me from on high

TURN THE PAGE
IN YOUR LIFE

BASED ON...
Day 155

Based on who says what,
credence is given to what can be done;
Based on a greater will,
my rising will soon come

Based on the Word,
I incessantly believe;
Based on Who I serve,
His gift I receive

WHEN I LOOK
Day 156

There's so much more
than the naked eye can see;
There's a wondrous future
that eagerly awaits me

There's so much more
than can be captured in a book;
Doing far better than before
when I look

TURN THE PAGE
IN YOUR LIFE

GET THE FEELING
Day 157

Everything is alright
and I am feeling good;
I made it through another night
when some didn't think I would

Everything is really fine
and I am feeling in a special way;
I'm blessed to be alive
knowing I've been favored another day

LONG AGO
Day 158

There was something in work
before I ever arrived on the scene;
There was a planned design of me
and on my life would be a lien

I am prohibited from being available
just to be condemned;
Long ago I was valued as priceless,
accepted and protected as His begemmed

TURN THE PAGE
IN YOUR LIFE

95

THINGS SEEM SO PERFECT
Day 159

Things seem so perfect,
I'm not giving place to the negative;
I will magnify the good around
as I amplify positive words in sound

Things seem so perfect,
I'm not focusing on what is wrong;
I will maintain the hope I have
through word and song

I JUST DON'T KNOW
Day 160

The greater comes about
at a price to pay;
It's not to be taken for granted,
nor is it meant for play

When I reach that point,
to the world I will show;
You have to stand strong
in the face of "I just don't know"

TURN THE PAGE
IN YOUR LIFE

WHAT'S OUTSIDE?
Day 161

Been inside all day,
watching through the windows;
Thinking about that day,
when I can travel the plains and plateaus

For now, I'll enjoy the sunshine
and others going about their way;
Outside I will be soon to join,
goodbye to this hospital stay

TOGETHER
Day 162

We make a great team,
we've shared the same dream;
Everyday we've walked side by side,
talking openly, nothing to hide

We've come thus far
and it will continue forever;
Nothing can separate us
from being together

TURN THE PAGE
IN YOUR LIFE

HAD TO BE
Day 163

The inevitable
cannot be deterred;
A miracle to be seen by all,
shall also be heard

No one to take the credit for
what everyone is about to see;
Soon all will know and proclaim,
"Him, it had to be!"

MY WEAKNESS
Day 164

My weakness is my strength,
"Faith" is its name;
I have it not in myself
but in Him lies the blame

This weakness is good,
not something I can live without;
It leads to hope and trust in Him,
a detour from the common route

TURN THE PAGE
IN YOUR LIFE

PETRIFIED
Day 165

I'm too petrified,
to have any doubt;
I'm too ready,
to scream and shout;
Over that something good,
on the verge to come;
I will await in faith,
inviting others to get some

OUT OF THE SHADOW
Day 166

I was covered
with a shadow of fear;
I was covered,
unable to see clear

I was covered,
left to feel;
I was covered wrongfully,
until You were revealed

TURN THE PAGE
IN YOUR LIFE

OBJECTION
Day 167

"Objection" rang loudly
throughout the courtroom;
The false evidence at hand
suggested that I was doomed

However, it was all a setup
for the truth to be told;
"You are now set free,"
the Judge proclaimed loud and bold

WE TALKED
Day 168

We talked about the
What if?
How come?
How long?
How strong?
When will it all cease?
No guarantee of time
in this suffering of mine
but I shall trust and remain
steadfast in His perfect peace

TURN THE PAGE
IN YOUR LIFE

IT IS POSSIBLE
Day 169

A sea has been divided
A giant slain
Deliverances from prisons
A nation saved by posts with blood stains

Many reasons to give up,
because of seeing chances as probable;
I serve a God who is known
for doing the impossible

NOTHING FURTHER
Day 170

When there's nothing further
the doctor can do
and family and friends
take the word as final and true

They've only reached the limit
of where their hopes were lain;
Whereas I believe the report
for which the lamb was slain

TURN THE PAGE
IN YOUR LIFE

BREAKTIME
Day 171

Breaks are good,
much needed are they;
We have to rest,
not be so busy throughout the day

Breaks are the timeouts
our bodies need;
Let's take a moment to
relax, meditate and calmly breathe

CAN I GET A WITNESS?
Day 172

If it's been done before,
it can be done again;
Not necessarily the same,
but a win is a win

I'm willing to be His impossible
and with this sickness I qualify;
Can I get a witness?
God's will is that I live, not die

TURN THE PAGE
IN YOUR LIFE

LIVE WITH
Day 173

You are who I
want to live with
You are who I
find life worth living for
You are who I
want to grow old with
You are who
I find as my heart's core
You are who
I choose to live with forever more

ALWAYS WITH YOU
Day 174

Never too far away,
within a short distance;
I can reach you right away,
have your ear to listen

I'll never leave you alone,
no matter how it seems;
I'm always with you,
whether awake or in your dreams

TURN THE PAGE
IN YOUR LIFE

OWN THE MEMORIES
Day 175

We've made them
We own them
We are them
More valuable than any gem

Memories of the past
Memories that will last
Memories amassed
Memories forever unsurpassed

SIDE EFFECTS
Day 176

Faith treats the symptoms
Prayer gets to the root
What's left is believing,
accepting the truth

The side effect of healing
is having an inkling of doubt
You must trust and believe
He has completely worked it out

TURN THE PAGE
IN YOUR LIFE

OWNED
Day 177

Appreciate what you have,
its significance is what matters;
Others aren't meant to know
all that makes your heart patter

It could be the joy of present company,
or speaking to someone who has phoned;
You have a piece of them within,
as a cherished memory forever owned

NO DISCOUNT
Day 178

What I'm aiming for
is priceless to be asked
I'm in need of a miracle
so I come unmasked

What He has, He freely gives
no limit to the amount
All that's needed is unwavering faith
nothing more, nothing less, no discount

TURN THE PAGE
IN YOUR LIFE

MORE TIME
Day 179

No better moment than today,
to enjoy life to the fullest your way;
You can sit and ponder about many things,
whistle or hum many songs singers sing

Celebrate your changing beauty then and now,
with confidence and grace you say 'Wow!'
Have fun, relax, just do whatever is fine,
always live without regret of needing more time

WHAT A DEAL!
Day 180

My lot in life
is just as common as the next
The only difference is
heeding to the biblical text

It sets the standard
of operating beyond feel
With the reward of peace, love, and joy,
oh, what a deal!

TURN THE PAGE
IN YOUR LIFE

IT'S AMAZING!
Day 181

Love brought us together,
not the tragedy we both know;
Compassionate hearts,
knitted as colors of a rainbow

Friends for eternity,
preventing memories from ever fading;
Time is the factor,
keeping our bond beautifully amazing!

FIXED
Day 182

Some things in our lives
appear to be broken and unrepairable
leaving us feeling hopeless
enduring pain unbearable

Arise out of despair,
it's time to live life in the mix
Cast your burdens on Him
in exchange for the perfect fix

TURN THE PAGE
IN YOUR LIFE

VACATION
Day 183

In my thoughts,
I can escape to extravagant places;
Although my physical condition
attempts to contain me in certain spaces

In reality
I'm preparing for the ultimate manifestation
That grand day of being completely healed
and on my dream vacation

NO COMPARISON
Day 184

You can look around
and still find none greater
Who can speak healing to you?
The ultimate debater

There's no one as awesome
no one He'll shun
He is love and besides Him
there's no comparison

TURN THE PAGE
IN YOUR LIFE

EVERY MORNING
Day 185

Every morning,
I vow to live for today;
Every morning,
I release the bad news of yesterday

Every morning,
on my knees I pray;
Every morning,
my faith says today is the day

HOW MUCH?
Day 186

When it seems you're losing the battle
and may have had enough
Somewhere inside you're reminded
He loves me too much

I'm not worth Him giving up on
I surrender all I am for Him to touch
I will cling to Him with all I have
knowing the love He has for me is very much

TURN THE PAGE
IN YOUR LIFE

THE DRIVE HOME
Day 187

The backseat passenger
must appreciate the ride and enjoy the view;
Not doubting the driver's knowledge
of the route being taken through

The backseat passenger
must not get comfortable at frequent stops
in places unknown;
For the final destination to be revealed
is a mansion in the heavenly
that shall be called home

MY PREFERENCE
Day 188

Words are spoken
but not all are beneficial
You must know what to dispose of
and what to keep that's special

Weigh the pros and cons,
use His word as your reference
Meditate wisely on what He says,
letting it be your primary preference

TURN THE PAGE
IN YOUR LIFE

CONGRATULATIONS
Day 189

I have every reason to rejoice,
even during times of being counted out;
I have family, friends, and acquaintances
helping me overcome every crucial bout

I have every reason to rejoice,
without being under any prescribed medications;
My God has heard and answered,
affirmed by the angels shouting, "Congratulations!"

MY SECRET
Day 190

Unknown to many,
although revealed in the open,
is the secret for living
a successful life beyond hoping

Treat others well,
respect everyone the same;
The secret will soon widely spread
with honor when they speak your name

TURN THE PAGE
IN YOUR LIFE

WATER
Day 191

Water,
essential and priceless,
transparent,
Adaptable and niceness

Water,
flows to fill;
Such as we can be,
according to His will

INTO YOU
Day 192

So delighted You are here
as always dependable
Your company is precious
demonstrating nothing expendable

An impeccable character
pure, undefiled, admirable through and through
Oftentimes taken for granted by many
however, I'm choosing to be totally into You

TURN THE PAGE
IN YOUR LIFE

DO WHAT HE SAYS
Day 193

Stay strong,
it won't last always;
Know that
My promise surely pays

My word,
never unbelievably hysterical;
Do as I say,
they shall witness you as the miracle

THE NOTEBOOK
Day 194

Hope is written
in this book I have
Love is lived
through my life's path
'Keep moving' is heard
in my spirit
'Don't give up' is running
through my head
Failures of the past, don't look
Reflect only on the words in His notebook

TURN THE PAGE
IN YOUR LIFE

HE DIDN'T HAVE TO
Day 195

Every tear that I've ever cried,
was emptying me of foolish pride;
It took every bow on my knees,
to realize He paid the debt and hidden fees

What I had to give in return
was provided in the journey through;
Him alone to be glorified,
for doing what He didn't have to

ANY IDEA?
Day 196

'Why has this come upon me?'
I cry to myself when alone
What have I done to deserve this?
What was it I did that was so wrong?

My child, you're needed
to bring hope to the hopeless around
This is only for a moment
soon you'll be restored and unbound

TURN THE PAGE
IN YOUR LIFE

MY NEIGHBOR
Day 197

How am I doing?
I'm doing just fine;
Living each day to the fullest
no concern about time

Seeking what I can do or give
to someone as a show of favor;
Knowing that I will be rewarded,
based on how I treat my neighbor

HEARTBEAT
Day 198

The sound I hear
is that of life and love
The miracle that keeps us alive
orchestrated from high above

Forego not a day of giving thanks
for what you have, live, and eat
It all comes at the expense
of Him loving us from heartbeat to heartbeat

TURN THE PAGE
IN YOUR LIFE

LIVING THROUGH THE PAIN
Day 199

The heartaches will come,
all will seem to prevail;
There is something you should know,
in Him there is no fail

You will lose many tears,
like a down pouring of rain;
You must keep your faith,
He's living with you through the pain

SO COMPELLING
Day 200

I'm compelled to share with you
the evidence which I found
It supports the word
that can loose anyone held bound

There's a King on high
Who's the Almighty of heaven and earth
Believing and accepting Who He is
to your life will bring much worth

TURN THE PAGE
IN YOUR LIFE

JUST VISITING
Day 201

I'm just a voyager,
traveling an unknown course;
I'm just trusting Him,
the one and only greatest force

No time to stop now,
walking this faith that's explicit;
I'm reassured by the sunrise,
how this life is just a visit

NO TIME FOR CRYING
Day 202

Standing against so much
that has come my way
Not sure if I could continue holding on
not for even one more day

Tears falling down my face
Fear torments with thoughts of dying
I'm then reminded of being a child of the Most High
time out for doubt and no time for crying

TURN THE PAGE
IN YOUR LIFE

SEASONED
Day 203

Why do bad things occur,
specifically to those doing good?
It is not my stress or concern,
after doing all I could

We each serve a purpose
and must live faith well-reasoned;
Ready for whatever comes,
no matter how it is seasoned

RUNNING
Day 204

Though I fall
I can still crawl
My hands and knees may ache
But my spirit won't break

No matter when I get there,
I'm reaching for the vision that's stunning
My healing in His care, therefore
I will continue crawling, walking, and running

TURN THE PAGE
IN YOUR LIFE

FEELING GOOD
Day 205

Thankful for this day,
readying to do what I could;
Allowing nothing to hold me back,
while I'm feeling this good

Using the life given me,
it'll be to His glory to do what I would;
It's by the power of His spirit,
that keeps me feeling this good

A NEW ME
Day 206

It's a fresh and exciting new day
Something special is in the air
So glad that goodness has come my way
No longer having a worry to bear

The report has been read
and it says that I'm doing better than expected
I had no doubt of what was said
my faith caused the bad to be intercepted

TURN THE PAGE
IN YOUR LIFE

KNOWN BY YOU
Day 207

"Who am I?"
is the question I sometimes ponder;
Created in Your image
as an awesome wonder

I'm encouraged
with the knowledge of what is true;
I have a purpose that begins with
being known by You

RIGHT OF PASSAGE
Day 208

Trust, believe,
know that He is able
Accept the invitation
to feast at His table

No greater thing
has anyone done to deliver a message
He freely gives hope, love, peace
All we need is to take the right of passage

TURN THE PAGE
IN YOUR LIFE

GOOD THING
Day 209

To undeservingly have this day,
is more than a reason to sing;
It's Him continually blessing me
as the testimony of a good thing

My smile is shining brighter,
valued more than any gem or bling;
His presence in my life
is my most treasured good thing

WHEN YOU NEED
Day 210

Although I may appear down,
I still stand by your side
A friend in me you've found,
words spoken of love not pride

I am here for you
everyday indeed
Fighting against time for you
to call when you need

TURN THE PAGE
IN YOUR LIFE

WHAT FOR
Day 211

Cry?
No need;
Rejoice?
Indeed

Things are what they are,
yet, I believe He will restore;
"His will be done" is my answer to,
What for?

GOING UP
Day 212

Rising because I must
Rising because I can
Ain't letting anything keep me from living
my full lifespan

Every day I'm getting up
and going up to a higher place
To be shown in my living
reflected in the joy on my face

TURN THE PAGE
IN YOUR LIFE

TEST DRIVE
Day 212

Rejoice,
in being alive!
The trial you're enduring,
is but a test drive

Be humbly royal,
just as Jesus appeared riding the pony!
This will end
as your glorious testimony!

WRECKAGE
Day 213

You may not see it
but I've been through dreadful things
What stands before you now
is the wreckage that remains

To be alive and where I am today
was a journey I was destined to take
All of those past disasters served
to strengthen me for your sake

TURN THE PAGE
IN YOUR LIFE

EVEN BETTER
Day 214

The report may have said the worst,
but it's not the final word;
The doctors have done very well,
but my faith will not be deterred

There's a book written,
in it is a personal letter;
It simply reads,
"I've come to make all things better!"

JUST STARTING
Day 215

All things are new
I see clearly
Touching the hearts of those
who are near me

The support I've received,
not once was there any departing
Forever you are my friend,
ready for the journey ahead just starting

TURN THE PAGE
IN YOUR LIFE

YOUR CHOICE
Day 216

Why doubt?
Why weep?
Why be disturbed?
Why lose sleep?

Accept peace!
Use your voice!
You possess the power
of choice!

LORD
Day 217

Is there someone
greater than I?
Who reigns within me
yet sits on high?

I thank you for the peace
You bring
You are Lord above all
my reason to live and sing

TURN THE PAGE
IN YOUR LIFE

SOMETIMES
Day 218

Sometimes,
I've given you the worst of me;
Sometimes,
I've pained your heart in grief

Sometimes,
situations are but a breeze;
For throughout all time,
in you I'll believe

GOODNIGHT
Day 219

The days can be rough,
thoughts punishing
I'm encouraged to be tough
at times I feel my strength diminishing

In the quiet times,
I find restored power to fight
When I rest my mind,
I put tomorrow behind and say goodnight

TURN THE PAGE
IN YOUR LIFE

COMPASSION
Day 220

Being present when needed
Lending a hand to lift
Your compassion
is God's operative gift

Giving of your time,
providing what's needed from your hand;
It illustrates His compassion,
clearly for all to understand

MY TEAM
Day 221

When I'm down in the dumps,
treating others bad,
caring more about myself,
less about you feeling sad;
I ask your forgiveness
I know you'd probably want to scream
Yet you accept my apology
reminding me we're all on the same team

TURN THE PAGE
IN YOUR LIFE

LONE SURVIVOR
Day 222

A rugged road I've traveled,
to arrive at my destination near You;
Having weathered the storms of life,
I was determined to make it through

Now that I'm safe from harm,
with You as my everlasting provider;
No more shall I see myself as,
"The Lone Survivor"

ALL I HAVE
Day 223

Air that I breathe
words that I speak
I give it all to You
whether I'm feeling strong or weak

You deserve it all
and so much more
All I have I surrender to You
as I lay prostrate on the floor

TURN THE PAGE
IN YOUR LIFE

THE RIDE
Day 224

In life, sometimes we are hitched to difficulties,
as in marriage with a groom and bride;
But, through the good and bad,
we must be thankful for the ride

We are to share and learn from experiences,
they are treasures not meant to hide;
Only then can it make an impact,
for the next one having to take the ride

START TO FINISH
Day 225

The beginning was rough
but it's all coming to an end
I'm grateful for everyone
supporting all they can

As the finish nears,
vaporizing my fears
I can now wipe away my tears
and join in with the cheers

TURN THE PAGE
IN YOUR LIFE

WHAT'S HAPPENING IS
Day 226

What's happening is,
I'm on the verge of being made anew;
You may not physically see it now,
but soon to come is the breakthrough

What's happening is,
I stay encouraged and rejoice within;
It presses out what doesn't belong,
by the wondrous power of my Friend

FINDING HOPE
Day 227

Finding hope
is worth having to hang onto
Knowing there's a chance
for others to enjoy more of you

Becoming hope
to inspire others along the way
Makes the battle worth fighting,
this is our faith in action as we pray

TURN THE PAGE
IN YOUR LIFE

STUDYING THE BEST
Day 228

There have been many before me,
who have borne much heavier burdens;
Nonetheless,
they were at peace with a future certain

I'm reminded of them,
when seeking His rest;
Knowing He anointed each of us
to erase doubts by studying the best

LESS STATIC
Day 229

Clarity comes
in the peacefulness of time
You get to gather your thoughts
and de-stress your mind

The report given
I take as no more than static
But a word of healing from on high
I fully accept as vatic

TURN THE PAGE
IN YOUR LIFE

THREE WORDS
Day 230

We have words
that inspire us all;
Some are clichéd,
yet, they may prevent a fall

The three words I have for you,
are a prosperity message of wealth;
May God bless you abundantly
with "Extraordinary Priceless Health"

JUMPING
Day 231

Getting out in front
of what's trying to keep you behind
is what you have to do
to maintain a peace of mind

Jumping forward
is the way to go
Once the hurdle is cleared
then you can grow

TURN THE PAGE
IN YOUR LIFE

MEANINGFUL
Day 232

Loving me as I am,
is so wonderful;
Cheering by my side,
it's so beautiful

What more can I ask for?
Your love is amazingly plentiful;
You are my breath
for living life so meaningful

WHY DON'T YOU?
Day 233

Why don't you cry?
Why don't you show the pain?
You keep so much inside
where there is no gain

No need to cry,
when I've been prepared beforehand
No need to show any pain
I have peace in what He's given me to understand

TURN THE PAGE
IN YOUR LIFE

IN CHARGE
Day 234

To be afraid,
is not something I comprehend;
How to be a champion,
is what I understand

My weaknesses and fears
have all been loaded on a barge;
Sailed far away,
because I'm in the hand of Who's in charge

SEVEN DAYS
Day 235

Days one and two,
it hit me like a ton of bricks
Days three and four,
I had no hope of getting over it

Days five and six,
I turned to the Lord for an answer
Day seven came,
He assured me He's greater than cancer

TURN THE PAGE
IN YOUR LIFE

OWN IT
Day 236

You can let it go,
or you can hold on;
You can stand in faith,
or in fear, run

Though you may be weary
and ready to quit;
Remember it's His to bear,
so you don't have to own it

THE LIFE I KNOW
Day 237

Would it ever be known,
the life I know to live?
How can it be shown?
Through what I have to give?

I will share the love I have,
not out of pretense or for show;
I will define my purpose,
by living the godly life I know

TURN THE PAGE
IN YOUR LIFE

WHAT'S LEFT
Day 238

Prayers have been prayed,
my knees are sore;
I've sat through the counseling
and so much more

It's time that I
move aside myself;
Completely trust in Him,
because it's all I have left

MORNING TRAIN
Day 239

I'm standing at the gate
daring to be late
Don't wanna miss my ride
my rolling tide

There's a train coming
Due to arrive early in the morning
I have a reserved seat
Destination faith street

TURN THE PAGE
IN YOUR LIFE

STATE OF MIND
Day 240

I can think about
the worst that could happen;
I can tremble behind the door of fear,
listening to negative voices rapping

My knowing is worth
much more than what I think;
Therefore, I know
I shall rise and not sink

BE WITH ME
Day 241

You are here,
a trusted friend;
Unfailing love,
in you there is no pretend

I thank you
for all you've shown to see;
I'm forever grateful
of your choosing to be with me

TURN THE PAGE
IN YOUR LIFE

LIVE IN MY WORLD
Day 242

It's where love abounds
happiness is everyday
It's where peace is found
troubles are passed away

It's a place where all are welcomed
man, woman, boy or girl
No matter the age or race
I welcome you to live in my world

GIVE GOD
Day 243

I could give you my testimony,
which may provide hope for some;
I could give you inspirational stories,
that may help you overcome

Instead, I choose to give
what many trample as sod;
Yet, it's more priceless than the universe,
I give you the word of God

TURN THE PAGE
IN YOUR LIFE

ABOVE AVERAGE
Day 244

Without hope,
there is no reason to continue on
Sporadic beliefs
for a moment, keeps one strong

What is offered,
for gaining positive leverage,
is a life of faith in the One
Who's able to do exceedingly above average

PROMISING
Day 245

The words that are written,
encourage my soul
The words that are spoken,
make me whole

The Living Word of truth
is beyond mind-boggling
That same Word which died for me
remains promising

TURN THE PAGE
IN YOUR LIFE

THINGS GET CRAZY
Day 246

How the day goes,
can at times be very hectic
How it is perceived,
is nothing short of eclectic

In the midst of chaos,
allow your life to bloom like a spring daisy
Keep your cool and maintain control
to withstand when things get crazy

GET ON THE ROAD
Day 247

The road to recovery
is what I am on
Some days are tough
but I keep moving along

Better it is
to be able to travel
Rather than losing hope
having a mind that unravels

TURN THE PAGE
IN YOUR LIFE

BACK TO YOU
Day 248

Never too far gone,
where I've given up on us
We are spiritually mended as one,
despite my occasional lack of trust

Thankfully there's a route
that your love safely guides me through
In your embracing arms,
as I make my way back to you

DON'T SAY GOODBYE
Day 249

The words we speak
are said to last forever
What I wish to hear from you
is positive always, negative never

Let not our days lived
be in vain with a sigh
Remember the fun shared
from our lips never say goodbye

TURN THE PAGE
IN YOUR LIFE

I DO NEED YOU
Day 250

A personal touch you bring
makes every day anew
A special place in my heart
occupied and true

The thought of Your non-presence
causes a grave issue
My strength, joy, and smile
I realize I do need you

MIRACLES
Day 251

What you are to me,
I hope to be to you
By my side you've been,
through and through

Your caliber
is one of a kind
My miracle you are
in my heart defined

TURN THE PAGE
IN YOUR LIFE

I HAVE TO LET YOU KNOW
Day 252

There's something great
that must be told;
It's too awesome
to sit and hold

I'm feeling better than ever,
ready to get on the go;
I've been shown mercy
so, I have to let you know

TURN TO YOU
Day 253

Feeling down,
don't know why;
Searching everywhere
to catch a high

Days seem so long,
before I forget what to do;
I'll recapture my peace
as I turn to You

TURN THE PAGE
IN YOUR LIFE

AS LONG AS I'M AROUND
Day 254

As long as I'm around,
know that you have a chance
to make life what it is meant to be
not something lived in one glance

As long as I'm around,
know that you are loved for who you are;
Even when I'm physically gone,
know that I'm spiritually never too far

CAN'T EXPLAIN
Day 255

Stranger things
can't always be explained
Although we wish
to live a life that is made plain

The beauty of not knowing
is the surprise that awaits
Behind the curtain is hidden
something called glorious fate

TURN THE PAGE
IN YOUR LIFE

FROM THIS MOMENT
Day 256

From this moment
I know what matters
Appreciation of others
More than things or flatters
The glimpse of a smile
Memories as a child
Hearing the tweets of a bird
Grateful for sight not blurred
Upon me is this the grace bestowment
Peace, love, and joy from this moment

I STILL LOVE YOU
Day 257

How can one forget
the days of old?
Growing up, hanging out
living a life with no hold

Chasing dreams together,
because our friendship was true;
Keep it in your heart forever
just how much I still love you

REALISTICALLY SPEAKING
Day 258

Realistically speaking,
I am doing much better;
Floating on cloud nine,
away from illness, the debtor

Realistically speaking,
what is to come is for my good;
I am an example of positivity,
exemplifying the little engine that could

AFT TO FORWARD
Day 259

Looking back at life
I see the troubles I've overcome
Many were brought on by my own doing
leaving me to blame no one

As I look forward in my life
I can only hope to live the change I've become
Representing strength and joy
after long fought victories won

TURN THE PAGE
IN YOUR LIFE

CRITICAL MOMENT
Day 260

Emergency assistance is needed
Things are looking improbable
Time for family and friends to gather
Please pray for the impossible

During the critical moment,
faith is tested for assurance
Overcoming the affliction,
is only done through endurance

WALK WITH ME
Day 261

Alongside me
is where I need you to be
What I'm having to endure
is such a tragedy

I know I will be just fine
and things made much better than used to be
As long as
I have you to walk with me

TURN THE PAGE
IN YOUR LIFE

ALL THE LITTLE THINGS
Day 262

Your visits, hugs, kisses,
and attention you give to me
are much appreciated
with love unconditionally

The little things
we so often take for granted
become fruitful trees
within the hearts planted

HURT FEELINGS
Day 263

I may say some things
that hurt your feelings
It is no excuse for me to use
that with which I'm dealing

I apologize
for every word spoken in err
Will you forgive me,
so we can both move pass the hurt?

TURN THE PAGE
IN YOUR LIFE

BEYOND AND ABOUT
Day 264

The newness of mind
The freshness of life
I was born with a set time
I have a purpose to thrive

I'm going beyond the expectations
placed on me
I'm moving about living life
It's the proof I'm free

MY WHOLE LIFE THROUGH
Day 265

Let not the sorrows you have for me
become your memories
Let not the unrest within your soul
become your life summary

My whole life through
has a purpose far-reaching
It is not to bring anyone down
I take the precious moments as a teaching

TURN THE PAGE
IN YOUR LIFE

WHERE YOU ARE
Day 266

I've heard much talk about You
Where are You now?
I've known people to give their lives
for You to deliver them somehow

Here I am standing by your side
comforting you through family and friends
Here I am working through it all on your behalf
as evidenced by the medical hands

INSTANTANEOUS RECOVERY
Day 267

Something miraculous happens
when you come to the end of your rope
when you proclaim you've had enough
and realize He truly is your only hope

At that moment,
there is an awesome discovery
You are fully restored by faith,
the result is an instantaneous recovery

TURN THE PAGE
IN YOUR LIFE

POWER DRIVEN
Day 268

Strength not of my own
is pressing me forward
Could it be the prayers from you all
of healing, you're pushing me toward

When there's a multitude
praying and cheering for your living
A release begins to take place
that is spiritually power driven

LITTLE DID I KNOW
Day 269

Little did I know,
while I was asleep
you were praying over me
Little did I know,
during your visits
you sacrificed time and money for me
Little did I know,
whenever we talked
you were speaking life to me
Little do you know,
how grateful I am for you

TURN THE PAGE
IN YOUR LIFE

URGENT CARE
Day 270

It's urgent that I let you know
I appreciate you
For the many sacrifices made
to see me through

It's urgent that I let you know
I'm glad you were there
Tomorrow isn't promised
so I thank you today for your care

SENSIBLE
Day 271

Why does anyone need support?
Why should we have hope?
Why must we have a bleak forecast?
Why can't we find peace to cope?

It's sensible to have help standing
It's sensible to believe for the best
It's sensible to prepare for a better tomorrow
It's sensible to enjoy a peaceful rest

TURN THE PAGE
IN YOUR LIFE

TAKE A LOOK INSIDE
Day 272

What is hidden,
oftentimes is meant to be shared
There's a world around
needing a touch of love and care

The challenge is for you to
take a look inside
Don't be afraid to allow
your love and their need to collide

GIVE LOVE
Day 273

There's so much
fear going around
So much hate
covering ground

It's past time
we stop putting it above
what we should be giving
which is Love

TURN THE PAGE
IN YOUR LIFE

I DO FOR YOU
Day 274

What you expect from me
I'll go above and beyond
You mean the world to me
Together we share a special bond

I do for you
Just because
I do for you
That's what love does

LIFE ANEW
Day 275

New meaning for living
has come my way
New ways of giving
freely everyday

I am basting in the joy
of being an overcomer
I'm willingly sharing hope
so that you too may be an awesome wonder

TURN THE PAGE
IN YOUR LIFE

UNRESTRAINED
Day 276

I give up the fears
that have been holding me back
I give up the voices
that lead me off track

The positives I accept
poured down like rain
I'm now ready to arise
completely unrestrained

JOYFULLY CRYING
Day 277

Tears of freedom
I gladly cry out
Speechlessly amazed
how it came about

Without me knowing
the time nor day
It happened unexpectedly
all by His grace

TURN THE PAGE
IN YOUR LIFE

SEEMS TO ME
Day 278

Seems to me,
there should always be a reason to smile
Life is within limits of time
We must learn to enjoy it during this while

Seems to me,
we have the power of change searched for
Let's unlock the goodness inside
so that it may freely flow through our heart's door

STUPEFIED MIRACLES
Day 279

There are miracles
that confuse those who refuse to believe
Still there's no denying
how real they are by the ones who receive

People can think what they want
and believe what they must
I choose to be the stupefied miracle,
in Him continuing to trust

TURN THE PAGE
IN YOUR LIFE

ON COURSE
Day 280

Keep praying, keep hoping,
are words I'm repeatedly told
Keep trusting, keep believing,
make sure you're being bold

What it takes to be on course
may seem odd in doing at first
In due time, all will be much better
In the past will be the worse

MY HOPE IN YOU
Day 281

Having no other place to turn
I must now practice what I've learned
Hoping the bridge isn't burned
where I can't ask for what I haven't earned

I'm laying it all out
in faith and truth
I humbly submit and return
my hope in You

TURN THE PAGE
IN YOUR LIFE

LIVING FOR THIS CAUSE
Day 282

Thoughts of what is there to live for
somehow creep into my mind
Reminiscing on all the wrong in life
and how this world can be so unkind

The truth then pierces my soul
as I take a pause
My purpose of existence is reason enough
in living for this cause

ANCHORED FAITH
Day 283

I've been swayed
pulled in every direction
Thinking I knew it all
rejected any correction

Then the winds had blown me off course
to hold me steady I had no weight
I made the emergency call
and there You were to anchor my faith

TURN THE PAGE
IN YOUR LIFE

HAVING SEEN YOU
Day 284

I know it's been hard
for you to come see me like this
I understand you staying away
choosing rather to sit and reminisce

I'm overjoyed that you've decided
to spend this time with me
Seeing you really does my heart good
your presence is appreciated most certainly

YOU'LL SEE
Day 285

Be not in despair
There's more going on than you perceive
This is just a lot in life,
not something you should prepare to bereave

The ending to this story
will be the beginning of something great
Don't give up too soon,
you'll see His timing is never too late

TURN THE PAGE
IN YOUR LIFE

I KNOW FOR SURE
Day 286

To be sure of something
there mustn't be any doubt
Whatever in life that's going on,
know that it can be worked out

Family and friends are positioned to help
so that nothing's a blur
Helping to establish a person's hope in tomorrow
one that may be lived for sure

SECONDS COUNT
Day 287

When time is wasted
regrets are made
Dear ones can soon be gone
many left dismayed

Make every second count
for every minute and hour of the day
Share the love all around,
capturing memories worthy of replay

TURN THE PAGE
IN YOUR LIFE

MY PROVIDER
Day 288

Whatever the need,
I've never lacked
You've supplied every time,
not once keeping track

I thank You much and always,
my Provider You are
I gladly present all I have to you,
a satisfaction to my heart

LOVE HAS A MEANING
Day 289

In all my years of living
the one thing I've learned and know
The meaning of love
in word and deed, You show

Having You is a positive addiction,
I'm happy to announce
You're what makes the world better,
we can use every ounce

TURN THE PAGE
IN YOUR LIFE

WHAT IT IS TO BE YOURS
Day 290

Having love
Having peace
Having a life
That kept my heart at ease

Words of wisdom
I sat before You gleaning
What it is to be Yours
is simply to have meaning

SETTING ME UP
Day 291

Praying
enhanced my trust
Strength
helped me to stand up

Love brought me to you

Faith
replaced all luck
All along
You were setting me up

TURN THE PAGE
IN YOUR LIFE

162

MY BACKUP PLAN
Day 292

Where I am
was purposed to be
It's a road I'm to travel
without familiarity

I have this feeling
things will be fine, although out of my hand
I have the support of friends like you
as my backup plan

GRASPING AT HOPE
Day 293

Needing something or someone
to hold onto
I was at a place in life
and didnt know what to do

Family and friends came near,
and began helping me to cope
No longer am I weary from
grasping at hope

TURN THE PAGE
IN YOUR LIFE

JUST FOR AN HOUR
Day 294

For you to give an hour
really brightens my day
I'm elated by your presence
Sure wish that longer you could stay

What's found in you
is an affectionate power
Reviving my soul from drought
sustaining me until that next hour

FAITH, MOST VALUABLE RESOURCE
Day 295

What do I need
to get your attention?
What would it take
for you to listen?

I heard Your voice
in an answer that put me on course
Faith is all it takes
it's the most valuable resource

TURN THE PAGE
IN YOUR LIFE

CLEAR DIRECTION
Day 296

There is no road we travel
that is of perfection
In learning lessons of life
we must encounter obstacles and rejections

However, there are those
whom He speaks through for our correction
Family, friends, and even foes
He uses to give us clear direction

STRONG INSPIRATION
Day 297

It shall come to pass
this I know
I'm very confident of the happy ending
to this show

The faith is strong within
unmovable
It's my inspiration for receiving the positive
unimaginable

TURN THE PAGE
IN YOUR LIFE

TAKING YOUR HAND
Day 298

Being an expert
at doing it all myself
Never saw the day coming
when I must rely on someone else

It only strips the pride
and changes my plan
It was never meant for me to fight alone
I'm gladly taking your hand

CLOSE TO YOU
Day 299

Before what has become
we've always been tight as glue
Nothing in this world
was ever allowed to divide us two

In the toughest of times
together we fought through
Very glad you're my best friend
forever I will remain close to you

TURN THE PAGE
IN YOUR LIFE

NEW MESSAGE
Day 300

Moaning and groaning
in such grief
Searching and praying
for some relief

A soft voice I heard
speaking only what I could manage
I surrendered and gave it to the Father
knowing it was to my advantage

NEGOTIATIONS
Day 301

Having those who care
surrounding me
can make the difference
in the outlook I see

For my good
they make better the situation
Their love comes undeniably
without negotiation

TURN THE PAGE
IN YOUR LIFE

POLEMICS
Day 302

I've been given the polemic
against fiery trials
The words are powerful
and carried with me each spiritual mile

They tell me
the testings won't last always
They're only designed to strengthen me
ahead for greater days

BREATHE
Day 303

It's easy to breathe
when you have much to believe in
Your days become brighter
The load carried seems lighter

You come to know
just how fully alive you are
You stand up
moving from beyond the dark

TURN THE PAGE
IN YOUR LIFE

LOOK AROUND
Day 304

There's much to live for
when you open your eyes to take notice
Many who care and pray for you
which is only sad when you don't know this

You're the reason for their gathering,
the reason for lost love being found
No longer walk in blindness
appreciate all as you take a look around

ARE YOU THERE?
Day 305

I can't feel You with my hands
Are you there?
I feel a warmth like embracing arms
I know You care

I can't see You with my eyes
Are You there?
Yet, I admire Your presence
in answering my prayer

TURN THE PAGE
IN YOUR LIFE

HEAR MY PLEA
Day 306

I need help
willing to accept it from anyone
I'm in a dim place in life
feeling all alone, empty handed, and undone

Oh, what I'd give
to rise again and break free
Lord, I'm asking You to
Please, hear my plea

NOTHING SHORT
Day 307

It's a miracle
that I'm alive today
Thankful for family and friends
and those I met along the way

Amazing grace helped me
escape with my life, avoiding an abort
All because of steadfast faith and prayers
nothing short

TURN THE PAGE
IN YOUR LIFE

BEHIND THE SCENES
Day 308

What's going on?
Like a puppet, it feels like strings are attached to me
I'm doing what I can on my own
although I'm feeling low on energy

That which is keeping me afloat
fills me with vitality as though I was a teen
It's the heavenly One living inside of me
doing all the work behind the scenes

EPIDEMIC
Day 309

There's something going around
that many need to contract
It can surely make a difference
in what one says and how one acts

Once you have it
you'll be fulfilled by what you've been missing
It's the ultimate epidemic
that'll positively change your entire way of living

TURN THE PAGE
IN YOUR LIFE

SEISMIC
Day 310

There's a seismic tremoring
taking place within
Fear is crumbling, doubt is fading
I'm starting to believe I can win

Unstoppable
is the place I'm moving into
Ready to show who's boss
as I accept healing as true

BEFITTING
Day 311

It's wonderful and
so amazing to witness
the miraculous power of the will
taking care of business

Not my will
but the One Who is on the throne sitting
He rises on behalf of His children
to bestow that which is befitting

TURN THE PAGE
IN YOUR LIFE

THAT FEELING
Day 312

You often wonder
whether things will work out in time
You struggle within
to maintain a peaceful state of mind

Suddenly there's a feeling
that comes over you so strong
Preparing you for the breakthrough
from within, correcting all that's been wrong

AFFORDABLE CARE ACTS
Day 313

Helping someone in need
the best you can
Sharing what you have
without expectations of receiving from their hand

Generosity goes a long way
defying hopelessness as a fact
All it takes is what you're able to give
as an affordable care act

TURN THE PAGE
IN YOUR LIFE

TRUMPING
Day 314

Many say the impossible can't happen
this is their complacent cry
It may be true for them
but you'll never know unless you try

The odds may be against you
Yet, along the road you continue thumping
For the cards are in the Father's hands
He's prepared you for the trumping

SPOKEN FROM THE BUSHES
Day 315

I need you to go and deliver
My people
I know it seems difficult to do
battling illnesses of evil

You're going to be my example of healing
and for them you will give a push
Just remember My words
that have been spoken from the bush

TURN THE PAGE
IN YOUR LIFE

LINCOLNIC
Day 316

Seeking emancipation
within my soul
Tired and worn
from battling this thing of old

I am reminded that I am free
it was written in a book long ago
It's quite lincolnic for me
the shackles of sickness I now let go

BIDEN
Day 317

I am a fighter
prepared to scrap for my life
I receive from higher
the power to overcome all strife

The bully called cancer has been defeated
and in the character of Biden
my sleeves are rolled and shirt unbuttoned
I can now breathe, no more hiding

TURN THE PAGE
IN YOUR LIFE

KING
Day 318

The King comes in peace
to offer equality
to be the lifter of infirmities
doing so, humbly

The King stands with the people
quietly accomplishing the necessary
Never losing sight of loving everyone
putting unforgiveness in a casket to bury

X
Day 319

In balancing the scales
by any means necessary
do not allow sickness
to make your faith wary

At times you will feel alone
which makes things a little complex
But deep inside you have all you need
On your heart is placed an X

TURN THE PAGE
IN YOUR LIFE

CARING HANDS (ODE TO MOTHER TERESA)
Day 320

Not knowing why
but faith made a way
Bringing me to
make a difference in someone's day

With caring hands
I'll gladly do my part
To ensure all is made better
Doing my best to give someone a fresh start

DAD
Day 321

Making a way for me
ensuring all my needs were met
Always thinking of me
protecting me from every threat

Professing to me
your love even when things are going bad
To you I give my heart
and am ever proud to call you my dad

TURN THE PAGE
IN YOUR LIFE

MOM
Day 322

You've brought me into
this world with grace
You are the apple of my eye
everyone can see it on my face

You comfort me
without ever having a qualm
Forever you have my love
Forever I am grateful you are my mom

THE JOB
Day 323

It's not difficult to do
but tiresome it can be
The struggle is truly real
a fight worth being free

The success in overcoming
is through faith's door as I turn the knob
I'm entering in running
glad to successfully finish the job

TURN THE PAGE
IN YOUR LIFE

THEY NEED ME
Day 324

I can't go too far
for I am needed
Never will I give in
Never will I accept being defeated

I need you all
just as you need me
With so much to live for
humbly living this life I'll be

WHAT CANCER?
Day 325

I was told I had it,
something called cancer
When more tests were run,
they had no answer

It was gone
I was elated
A testimony of His mercy
I stood, not at all ill-fated

TURN THE PAGE
IN YOUR LIFE

THE BIG "C"
Day 326

Many were sad
because of me having the big "c"
I was perturbed
about them not knowing what it would be

It was an opportunity
for the bigger "C" to receive glory
and, so He did by crushing the big "c"
bringing a happy ending to my story

TAKE MY HAND
Day 327

Right here beside you
sitting in a chair
Awaiting your eyes to open
and see that I'm here

You turn and notice
that I'm with you, my friend
You extend appreciation with a smile
as I take your hand

TURN THE PAGE
IN YOUR LIFE

LET'S GO FOR A WALK
Day 328

Sometimes
you just have to get out
to see the sun
enjoy all that is around and about

Looking up to the sky
I stand and gawk
Mesmerized by the beauty of nature
I proceed to walk

BUT...
Day 329

I've been told
things are looking quite dim
I counter with,
"but you must know the greater Him!"

The doctors say chances are not
looking so good
But I know their predictions
do not speak for the Mighty One who could

TURN THE PAGE
IN YOUR LIFE

WASN'T IT YOU?
Day 330

For a while I've wondered,
"how did I make it thus far?"
I'd given up long ago,
having a lack of faith below par

Without any expectations,
I somehow pulled through
No credit taken for myself,
my Friend, I knew it was You

HAVING LIFE TO LIVE
Day 331

I must make the most
of this life I have to live
Sharing all of what I have
Yes, to others I freely give

Wanting the best for everyone
means I must forgive
This purposeful path I'm on
is how I'm choosing to lovingly live

TURN THE PAGE
IN YOUR LIFE

LOVE NEVER DIES
Day 332

Whether you know it or not,
it's there
Whether you give it or not,
it's clear

Time has come
for all to realize
With an open heart,
you can grasp that love never dies

STRONG IS A RIGHT
Day 333

Weakness comes about
by believing all the doubt
The time must arrive
for allowing faith to drive

The unimaginable
will begin to take flight
With faith as your strength
know that being strong is a right

TURN THE PAGE
IN YOUR LIFE

CLOSE THE DOOR
Day 334

Time has come
for you to close the door
Fear and failure
can no longer have control as before

A new life has been given
for you to take advantage of
One that has been groomed
and nurtured in love

THE WIND BEHIND US
Day 335

What's before you
will soon be in the past
Don't fret about the current report,
your health will overcome and outlast

Allow not the boisterous winds
to stress you and make fuss
Together we'll walk and focus on your future
putting the wind behind us

TURN THE PAGE
IN YOUR LIFE

MY SHOES
Day 336

Despite all I've encountered
I have some great news
I'm still able to run the race
in my faith-filled shoes

My shoes are custom made
to carry an allotted load
Specifically designed
for my God appointed road

IMPECCABLE
Day 337

My life has not been impeccable
Mistakes I've made along the way
Yet, I am always grateful
for being blessed with another day

His perfection
overshadows all my flaws
placing me in right standing
leading me as His Spirit draws

TURN THE PAGE
IN YOUR LIFE

Arkansas is Fighting Cancer One Poem a Day

BALDNESS IS BEAUTIFUL
Day 338

The loss of hair
at first, put me in a state of shame
Little was I aware
many others like me were the same

I was now part of the elite
set to overcome something very unique
Sporting it proudly now that I know
I fully accept baldness as beautiful

NO PRESSURE
Day 339

I refuse to give my strength
to increasing pressure
I'll stand my ground daily in faith
as it is made fresher

I will concentrate on positives
as my hope core
When it comes to negative pressure knocking,
I shall refrain from answering the door

TURN THE PAGE
IN YOUR LIFE

186

WEIGHTLESS
Day 340

What I have
is most powerful
Although you can't touch it
in the natural

Located within
It's an unstoppable greatness
The Spirit of Comfort
provided from on high and weightless

LET ME OUT
Day 341

The real me
lies beneath what you see;
Don't be tricked by your eyes,
examine with your soul my beauty

I struggle within myself
to erase all doubt;
Sure enough I hold faith,
my Savior will let me out

TURN THE PAGE
IN YOUR LIFE

TAKE ME HIGHER
Day 342

Always be ready
for whatever is to become of your life;
Treat others with respect,
be a peacemaker and deter any strife

Wear that beautiful trusting smile
and never distinguish your blessed fire;
For there will come a day
when you'll be taken gloriously higher

ONE MORE CHANCE
Day 343

Seeing me the way I am
is far from knowing who I am;
I keep praying and believing
I'll soon be out of this jam

I will have that moment
to experience life as more than a glance;
I will make everlasting memories
touching lives with one more chance

TURN THE PAGE
IN YOUR LIFE

TOO LATE TO GIVE UP
Day 344

Though the struggles have been
keeping me on bended knee;
It's brought me much closer to Him
than I ever thought I'd be

By now many would lose hope,
believing there's nothing else in the cup;
Look at the plate with the bread of life,
you'll realize it is too late to give up

THE MARINE
Day 345

Though undeserving at times,
I prayed for the lives of others;
Answering those prayers,
You've came and comforted like a mother

Not thinking about my own needs,
I continue on in life being playful;
I know those needs are met,
because You are "Always Faithful"

TURN THE PAGE
IN YOUR LIFE

THE AIRMAN
Day 346

Coming very far from above,
to meet us where we are;
He is the Almighty Conqueror,
Who's knocking to live in our hearts

The impossible being done,
in Him is where it begins;
He is our motivation
to "Aim High, Fly-Fight-Win"

THE SOLDIER
Day 347

The army of One,
Who can defeat all you ever encounter,
is also the One
Who created the universe as the founder

He's come to heal and make you whole
because He is a true friend;
Never to leave you stranded,
for you are the one "This He'll Defend!"

TURN THE PAGE
IN YOUR LIFE

THE SAILOR
Day 348

The sea roared boisterously,
yet it was tamed by His word;
Let Him be the captain of your ship,
the first you call, not second or third

He'll sail you safely through all waters,
positioning you where you belong;
Your ship will never run aground
as many testify to Him being "Always Strong"

BIG NOISE
Day 349

Why not make it known,
what has been done?
Once things were looking grim,
but now the battle has been won

Let this be encouragement
to all the girls and boys;
Be ready to ring that bell
and make the loudest noise

TURN THE PAGE
IN YOUR LIFE

IMPEACHED
Day 350

There's a terrible thing
that has come upon me;
I don't need to know how it happened,
but to be made free

From whence it came,
was clearly a security breach;
The council of prayer is setup,
to rid this cancer as impeached

MY DAY, MY DANCE
Day 351

Today is the day,
that I do a new dance;
Today is the day,
I move to certainty from chance

Today is the day,
that many witness what was concealed;
Me being a miracle,
a living testimony revealed

TURN THE PAGE
IN YOUR LIFE

NEVER LETTING YOU GO
Day 352

All things have an end,
but special moments are without time;
Like memories of precious friends
being there for you at the drop of a dime

The bond that was formed,
began only as we know;
Just rest assured that
I'm never letting you go

NEXT TO YOU
Day 353

I am safe,
no worry will overtake;
Next to You,
all doubt I forsake

I am anew,
made whole as a newborn;
Next to You,
my allegiance is sworn

TURN THE PAGE
IN YOUR LIFE

YOUR EYES SAY IT ALL
Day 354

I can believe whatever
I wish to believe;
Hope for whatever
I wish to receive

The assurance of getting
beyond this condition;
Is seeing myself through your eyes,
transformed from this position

IMPERVIOUS
Day 355

In Your hands I remain secure,
protected from what seeks to harm me;
In Your hands my provisions are met,
You're all I need to hear and see

Your Word guides me
into perfect peace
making me completely impervious
against any doubt someone speaks

TURN THE PAGE
IN YOUR LIFE

SHOUTING IT LOUD
Day 356

You are such a dear friend,
with me through it all;
Never too far away,
always protecting my fall

The one face
that will never get lost in a crowd;
You're what friends are made of,
I love you and am shouting it loud

LEANING ON YOUR WORD
Day 357

You said I can make it,
You said I have what it takes;
You said I have a higher calling,
all for goodness sake

I'm putting all my trust
in what I vividly heard;
Allowing You to lead,
as I lean on Your word

TURN THE PAGE
IN YOUR LIFE

GETTING TO KNOW YOU MORE
Day 358

If things weren't what they are,
would I be who I am?
If things were reversed,
could I have compassion on them?

Can't go back in time,
so I'm committed to making sure
my time is spent wisely,
in getting to know you more

LIVING FOR YOU
Day 359

You said if I care,
don't leave you now;
You told me to fight,
as best I know how

You're always there,
cheering me through;
If there's ever a greater reason,
it is living for you

TURN THE PAGE
IN YOUR LIFE

CAN'T LOOK BACK
Day 360

Moving ahead,
focused with a flint face;
Determined to reach
my appointed place

Not adding weight
to my deliverance sack;
My time is near,
farewell to looking back

WHAT A MOMENT
Day 361

Days like this,
don't last forever;
Must take advantage,
do something clever

Live life above
sickness as my opponent;
Live life spreading joy and love,
in this given moment

TURN THE PAGE
IN YOUR LIFE

THE HEALER
Day 362

I am where I am,
for reasons unknown;
Having to face something
I can't beat on my own

You are the healer,
with all power in Your hands;
With unwavering faith,
on Your word, I shall continually stand

SURRENDERING TO YOU
Day 363

In my life,
I did what I wanted to;
Now I'm at a loss for hope
and I'm running back to You

I surrender
all I am and have to give;
Asking You to hear
and grant me favor to live

TURN THE PAGE
IN YOUR LIFE

MY SECOND CHANCE
Day 364

The first time around,
things were going great;
Never gave a thought
to what was coming on my plate

Now I'm asking
for Your healing hands;
To touch and make me whole
with a second chance

CELEBRATING THIS
Day 365

A reason to sing,
is having to be alive today;
Lord, I'm thankful
of the path for me You lay

Without faith in You,
I'd be out of my wits;
Instead, I'm completely healed,
rejoicing and celebrating this

TURN THE PAGE
IN YOUR LIFE

FROM GENE, TO SHAUN

WHY NOT ME?

As the chaotic crescendo gives chase to melodic spasms,
my dreams become ensnared by ne'er do wells
panhandling for halos and cuties on the side of freeways
asking for any way to find no more pain

We sit questioning God again and again,
yet, ignoring His answers again and again
As the crescendo gives way to the chorus.
His will, God's will, stands before us.
I tremble in fear, in anger and despair.
It's unfair!

The disdain and distaste envelops my lips
as it makes its own way from my mouth,
my throat and stomach,
through its eruptive discourse.
It leaves—
Relief, but for a second
In between each heave, each breath.
I catch the words in my throat before they escape.

But everything else finds egress. Why not allow it to escape?
I think it! I've thought it. Just let it escape.
"Why me?"
"Why not me?"
Am I not the same as Sally or Sue?
Or Marilyn, or even you?
I know in my uniqueness, I am fearfully and wonderfully made.
I have been created in His own image.

.

Yet still, why not me? Keep me in prayer.
Keep me in your prayers as the crescendo gives way to the chorus.
I tremble no more, I fear no more. I know my Father
And I know he watches over me

~In Honor of Shaun Carter from Gene Carter~

FIGHT LIKE A GIRL

Because you fight like a girl
You live like a lady
Because I see you fighting, I'm not frightened of your tears.
Because I see your strength, I understand your fears.
Still, you command my faith, you're its pen, its brush, and song
It is your will to live, your fight that keeps me strong
Because I see you fighting, I keep from sight, my tears.
Because I see your strength, I've masked from you, my fears.
God's grace becomes your aura, His blessings, your armor and crown
It is your will to live, your fight, that's so profound.

~In Honor of Shaun Carter from Gene Carter~

Dr. Owen Watson

Read excerpts, get exclusive inside looks at exciting upcoming projects, interviews and photos.

www.drowenwatson.com

Email: hello@authorowenwatson.com